Ladybird Readers

Where Is the Click Beetle?

To access the audio and digital versions
of this book:

1 Go to www.ladybirdeducation.co.uk
2 Click "Unlock book"
3 Enter the code below

58sWeEcbg7

Notes to teachers, parents, and carers

The *Ladybird Readers* Beginner level helps young language learners to become familiar with key conversational phrases in English. The language introduced has clear real-life applications, giving children the tools to hold their first conversations in English.

This book focuses on the times of the day and the preposition "on".

There are some activities to do in this book. They will help children practice these skills:

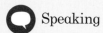 Speaking    Listening*   Reading

*To complete these activities, listen to the audio downloads available at **www.ladybirdeducation.co.uk**

Series Editor: Sorrel Pitts

Chants by Sorrel Pitts

LADYBIRD BOOKS

UK | USA | Canada | Ireland | Australia
India | New Zealand | South Africa

Ladybird Books is part of the Penguin Random House group of companies
whose addresses can be found at global.penguinrandomhouse.com.
www.penguin.co.uk   www.puffin.co.uk   www.ladybird.co.uk

Penguin
Random House
UK

Text inspired by *The Very Clumsy Click Beetle* by Eric Carle, first published in Great Britain by Hamish Hamilton, 1999
This version first published by Ladybird Books 2024
001

Printed in China

The authorized representative in the EEA is Penguin Random House Ireland, Morrison Chambers, 32 Nassau Street, Dublin D02 YH68

A CIP catalogue record for this book is available from the British Library

ISBN: 978-0-241-58763-8

All correspondence to:
Ladybird Books
Penguin Random House Children's
One Embassy Gardens, 8 Viaduct Gardens, London SW11 7BW

MIX
Paper | Supporting
responsible forestry
FSC® C018179
FSC
www.fsc.org

Ladybird Readers

Where Is the Click Beetle?

Inspired by
The Very Clumsy Click Beetle
by Eric Carle

It is morning!

The click beetle walks.

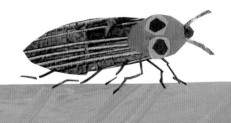

It is noon.

The click beetle is on
a flower.

It is afternoon.

The click beetle is on
the stones.

9

It is evening.

The click beetle is on
the grass.

It is night.

The click beetle sleeps.

Your turn!

1 **Talk with a friend.** 🗨

What time is it?

It is noon.

Where is the click beetle?

It is on the flower.

2 What is it? Listen. Circle the words.

1  (sun) flower

2  noon stones

3  flower grass

4  night tree

3 Read and clap!

It is morning. It is morning.
The click beetle walks.

It is noon. It is noon.
The click beetle is on a flower.

It is afternoon. It is afternoon.
The click beetle is on the stones.

It is evening. It is evening.
The click beetle is on the grass.

It is night. The click beetle sleeps.
It is night. The click beetle sleeps.